Alvar AALTO

Alvar Aalto

Alvar Aalto

teNeues

Editor in chief:
Paco Asensio

Editor and original texts:
Aurora Cuito

English translation:
William Bain

German translation:
Inken Wolthaus

French translation:
Michel Ficerai

Italian translation:
Giovanna Carnevali

Art direction:
Mireia Casanovas Soley

Graphic design / Layout:
Emma Termes Parera and Soti Mas-Bagà

Published worldwide by teNeues Publishing Group
(except Spain, Portugal and South-America):

teNeues Verlag GmbH + Co. KG
Am Selder 37, 47906 Kempen, Germany
Tel.: 0049-(0)2152-916-0
Fax: 0049-(0)2152-916-111

teNeues Publishing Company
16 West 22nd Street, New York, N.Y., 10010, USA
Tel.: 001-212-627-9090
Fax: 001-212-627-9511

teNeues Publishing UK Ltd.
Aldwych House, 71/91 Aldwych
London WC2B 4HN, UK
Tel.: 0044-1892-837-171
Fax: 0044-1892-837-272

teNeues France S.A.R.L.
140, rue de la Croix Nivert
75015 Paris, France
Tel.: 0033-1-5576-6205
Fax: 0033-1-5576-6419

www.teneues.com

Editorial project:

© 2002 **LOFT** Publications
Domènech 9, 2-2
08012 Barcelona. Spain
Tel.: 0034 93 218 30 99
Fax: 0034 93 237 00 60
e-mail: loft@loftpublications.com
www.loftpublications.com

Printed by:
Gráficas Anman. Sabadell. Spain

May 2002

Die Deutsche Bibliothek – CIP-Einheitsaufnahme
Ein Titeldatensatz für diese Publikation ist bei der Deutschen Bibliothek erhältlich.

ISBN: 3-8238-5583-25

Alvar Aalto was brought up in a family and cultural setting that extolled the Western humanistic traditions which, at the beginning of the twentieth century, consisted in the recovery of Classical and Renaissance values. At the same time, thanks to his father, who promoted projects for the correct exploitation of the natural environment, Aalto inherited a strict compromise with Finnish culture, with its careful respect for nature. The highly detailed study of the landscape, its measurement and description, established the perfect framework for developing the ability to contextualize and integrate buildings into the surroundings. This familiarity and experience with territory form the basis of Aalto's sensitivity for organic forms and natural materials.

In the nineteen-twenties the architect came into contact with the vanguards and with the innovating thought of the Bauhaus, establishing friendships with artists and critics, outstanding among which is that with Laszlo Moholy-Nagy. Many of the former's doctrines were adopted by Aalto as he became one of the maximum exponents of the flowering of modern architecture. Aalto was also to enrich his formal language by introducing organic references, constructive artisanal details, and a treatment of natural materials like stone or wood in an innovative way.

The fusion of new concepts and traditional techniques generated a timeless architecture that has come down to our own times without being overshadowed by the new trends. The work of Alvar Aalto continues to establish himself as a reference point for architects and designers the world over.

Alvar Aalto wuchs in einer familiären und kulturellen Umgebung auf, die die humanistischen Traditionen des Abendlandes verherrlichte, die zu Beginn des 20. Jahrhunderts in der Wiedereinsetzung der Werte des Klassizismus und der Renaissance seinen Ausdruck fand. Seinem Vater, der damals bereits Projekte für eine schonende Umweltbehandlung unterstützte, verdankt er seine enge Beziehung zur finnischen Kultur mit ihrer Achtung vor der Natur. Die sorgfältige Beobachtung der Landschaft, deren Vermessung und Beschreibung bildeten den perfekten Rahmen, um seine Begabung für die Einbindung und Integration von Gebäuden in ihre Umgebung zu entwickeln. Diese Vertrautheit und Erfahrung mit dem Boden waren die Grundlage der Sensibilität Aaltos für organische Formen und natürliche Materialien.

In den zwanziger Jahren nahm er Verbindung mit den Avantgardisten und der im Bauhaus entstandenen neuen Denkweise auf und knüpfte Freundschaften mit Künstlern und Kritikern, unter denen Laszlo Moholy-Nagy zu erwähnen ist. Aalto übernahm viele seiner Doktrinen und wurde zu einem der größten Exponenten der blühenden modernen Architektur. Er bereicherte die formellen Ausdrucksformen mit der Einführung organischer Referenzen, mit künstlerischen Baudetails und behandelte die natürlichen Materialien, wie z. B. Stein und Holz, auf eine ganz neue Art.

Durch das Verschmelzen neuer Konzepte und traditioneller Techniken entstand eine zeitlose Architektur, die bis in unsere Zeit hineinreicht, ohne dass neue Tendenzen ihren Schatten auf sie werfen konnten. Das Werk Alvar Aaltos verkörpert noch immer eine Referenz für Architekten und Designer in der ganzen Welt.

Alvar Aalto a été élevé dans un environnement familial et culturel en résonance avec les traditions humanistes occidentales qui, au début du XXème siècle, tendaient à recouvrer les valeurs classiques et de la Renaissance. Grâce à son père, soutien fidèle des projets d'exploitation équilibrée de l'environnement, il a parallèlement hérité d'un engagement étroit envers la culture finlandaise, si respectueuse de la nature. L'étude minutieuse du paysage, mesuré et décrit, a établi le cadre parfait pour développer la capacité à contextualiser et intégrer les édifices dans leur environnement. Cette familiarité et cette expérience du terrain ont posé les fondations de la sensibilité d'Aalto envers les formes organiques et les matériaux naturels.

Au cours des années vingt, il put entrer en contact avec les avant-gardistes et la pensée novatrice surgissant du Bauhaus, développant des amitiés avec artistes et critiques parmi lesquels Laszlo Moholy-Nagy. Aalto adopta nombre de leurs doctrines et se convertit en l'un des exposants majeurs de la florissante architecture moderne. Par surcroît, il enrichit son langage formel en introduisant références organiques et détails de construction artisanaux mais aussi en traitant les matériaux naturels, la pierre ou le bois, de manière novatrice. La fusion des nouveaux concepts et des techniques traditionnelles a généré une architecture atemporelle qui nous est parvenue sans être éclipsée par les nouvelles tendances. L'œuvre d'Alvar Aalto s'érige toujours en référence pour les architectes et les créateurs du monde entier.

Alvar Aalto creò attorno a sé un ambiente familiare e culturale che risaltava le tradizioni umanistiche occidentali, le quali, all'inizio del secolo scorso, consistevano nel recupero dei valori classici e rinascimentali. Allo stessoo tempo, grazie anche all'aiuto di suo padre che sosteneva i progetti che garantivano una corretta utilizzazione dell'ambiente, ereditò uno stretto compromesso con la cultura finlandese, molto rispettosa nei confronti della natura. Il minuzioso studio del paesaggio, le sue proporzioni e descrizioni, stabilirono un quadro perfetto per sviluppare l'abilità di contestualizzare e integrare gli edifici nel loro intorno. Questa familiarità e esperienza con il territorio delinearono la base della sensibilità di Aalto per le forme organiche e per i materiali naturali.

Negli anni Venti entrò in contatto con le correnti avanguardiste e con il pensiero innovativo dichirato della Bauhaus, tessendo amicizie con artisti e critici tra i quali si segnala Laszlo Moholy-Nagy. Aalto acquisì molte delle sue dottrine e divenne uno dei massimi esponenti della fiorente architettura moderna. Arricchì inoltre il suo linguaggio formale introducendo "referenze organiche", dettagli costruttivi artigianali e lavorando materiali naturali come la pietra e il legno in modo nuovo.

La fusione dei nuovi concetti con le tecniche tradizionali generò una architettura atemporale che è arrivata sino ai giorni nostri senza che le nuove tendenze la occultassero. L'opera di Alvar Aalto continua ad essere considerata una referenza per gli architetti e i disegnatori dei tutto il mondo.

Paimio Tuberculosis Sanatorium

Paimio, Finland
1929–1932
Photographers: M. Kapanen & Maija Holma / AAM

Finnish health programs progressed in a spectacular way in the nineteen-twenties and nineteen-thirties owing to the initiative of the local administrations to create an extensive network of sanatoriums for tuberculosis and institutions of mental health. From the beginning, Aalto interested himself in this institutional architecture and presented work at many competitions, although he won only that of the Paimio Sanatorium. His particular way of interpreting patient care was based on the close collaboration among doctors and architects, who had to work in the same direction to heal the sick. A good example of this interaction between the building and the medical arts is the Paimio chair, which incorporates a certain angle in the backrest to aid the patient's respiration. In spite of the fact that this new conception in health almost never convinced the competent authorities, the Paimio sanatorium became a prestigious healing center due in part to its architecture. The compound is made up of a wing for patients' rooms; another for a cafeteria; the kitchen and the other common rooms; and the intersection between the two wings, which centralizes vertical movements.

Das finnische Gesundheitswesen machte während der zwanziger und dreißiger Jahre dank der Initiative der lokalen Verwaltungsbehörden aufsehenerregende Fortschritte mit der Erstellung eines ausgedehnten Netzes von Sanatorien für Tuberkulosekranke und Instituten für Geisteskrankheiten. Aalto war von Anfang an an der Architektur dieser Einrichtungen interessiert und nahm an zahlreichen Ausschreibungen teil, obwohl ihm nur das Sanatorium von Paimio zugesprochen wurde. Seine besondere Art der Auslegung der Krankenpflege basierte auf der engen Zusammenarbeit von Ärzten und Architekten, die zur Gesundung der Patienten in die gleiche Richtung hin arbeiten müssen. Ein gutes Beispiel für die Wechselwirkung von Konstruktion und Medizin ist der Stuhl von Paimio, dessen Rückenlehne einen bestimmten Winkel aufweist, wodurch dem Patienten das Atmen erleichtert wird. Obwohl diese neue Auffassung des Gesundheitswesen nur selten die zuständigen Behörden überzeugt hat, wurde das Sanatorium von Paimio, zum Teil dank seiner Architektur, zu einem angesehenen Heilzentrum. Die Anlage besteht aus einem Gebäudekörper mit den Zimmern, in einem anderen befinden sich Café, Küche und sonstige gemeinschaftliche Bereiche und ein Verbindungsteil zwischen beiden gruppiert die Treppenanlagen und Aufzüge.

La santé a progressé de façon spectaculaire en Finlande au cours des années vingt et trente, grâce à l'initiative des administrations locales visant à construire un réseau étendu de sanatoriums pour les malades de la tuberculose et les institutions psychiatriques. Depuis ses débuts, Aalto s'est intéressé à cette architecture institutionnelle et s'est présenté à de nombreux concours, remportant uniquement celui du sanatorium de Paimio. Sa manière particulière d'interpréter les soins aux patients repose sur une stricte coopération médecins-architectes, devant travailler dans une direction commune pour soigner les malades. La chaise de Paimio constitue un bon exemple de l'interaction construction-médecine, incorporant un angle précis pour le dossier afin de faciliter la respiration du patient. En dépit de cette conception novatrice de la santé il ne put que rarement convaincre les autorités compétentes. Le sanatorium de Paimio s'est transformé en un centre de traitement prestigieux, en partie grâce à son architecture. L'ensemble est composé d'un volume de chambres, d'un autre volume abritant la cafétéria, la cuisine et des zones communes et de leur intersection centralisant les communications verticales.

La salute finlandese fece grandissimi progressi negli anni Venti e Trenta grazie ad una serie di iniziative promosse dalle amministrazioni locali e finalizzate alla costruzione di un'estesa rete di istituti per la cura della tubercolosi e dei disturbi mentali. Fin dal primo momento, Aalto si interessò molto a questa architettura istituzionale e si presentò a numerosi concorsi, sebbene alla fine si trovasse a vincere solo quello per il sanatorio di Paimio. La sua particolare forma di interpretare la cura dei pazienti si basava in una stretta collaborazione tra medici ed architetti, che avrebbero dovuto lavorare congiuntamente per riuscire a sanare i malati. Un buon esempio dell'interazione tra tecnica costruttiva e medicina è la sedia Paimio, dotata di una ben definita inclinazione dello schienale per facilitare la respirazione del paziente. Nonostante il fatto che questa innovatrice concezione della sanità quasi mai riuscì a convincere le autorità competenti, il sanatorio di Paimio divenne un prestigioso centro di cura proprio grazie, in parte, alla sua architettura. Il complesso è composto da un volume che alloggia le stanze, un altro che ospita caffetteria e la cuccina.

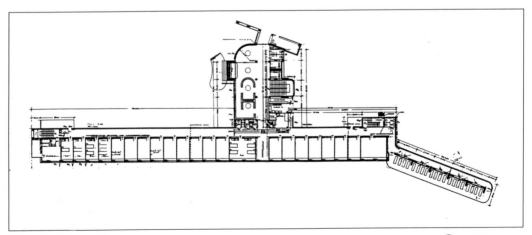

Type plan   Geschossgrundriss
Étage type   **Pianta Tipo**

0   2   4

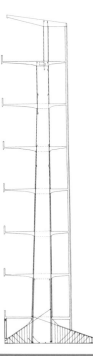

Structural scheme
Schema des Aufbaus
Schéma de la structure
Schema della Struttura

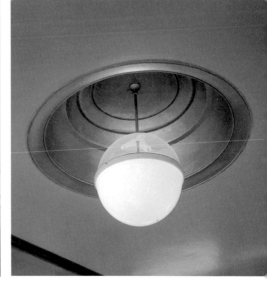

Viipuri City Library

Vyborg, Russia
1933–1935
Photographers: M. Kapanen / AAM

In 1927, Aalto won the competition for the Viipuri City Library. He began its design in 1933, but it was not until 1934 that he actually began its construction. The first sketches were clearly marked by classicist lines, but the project that was executed years later incorporated a new way of seeing the architecture and made it over into a masterpiece. The building comprises two elongated volumes that blend to create a common area that houses the entrance, the stairs (visible through a glassed front) and the vestibule to the auditorium, as well as some reading rooms and the children's library, which Aalto designed with special attention to the details. The lighting in the reading areas is by way of conical skylights that screen the light against brusque changes of illumination that would disturb readers. After the Second World War, the library was abandoned for ten years and thus underwent a marked deterioration. In 1992, the initiative to restore it came about, and the work is still continuing on the basis of donations from all over the world.

1927 gewann Aalto die Ausschreibung für die Bibliothek in Viipuri; und obwohl er 1933 mit den Plänen begann, wurde der Bau erst 1934 in Angriff genommen. Die ersten Entwürfe zeigten eindeutig klassizistische Tendenzen. Das später ausgeführte Projekt veranschaulichte jedoch eine neue Sicht der Architektur und wurde zu einem Meisterwerk. Das Gebäude besteht aus zwei länglichen Gebäudekörpern mit einem gemeinschaftlichen Bereich für den Eingang, die Treppen, die durch eine verglaste Fassade zu erkennen sind, und eine Vorhalle zum Auditorium, zu einigen Lesesäle und zur Kinderbibliothek, bei der Aalto ganz besonderen Wert auf die Details legte. Die Beleuchtung der Lesebereiche erfolgt über kegelförmige Oberlichter, die das Licht dämpfen, so dass die Leser nicht geblendet oder durch plötzliche Lichtwechsel gestört werden. Nach dem Zweiten Weltkrieg war die Bibliothek zehn Jahre verlassen, wodurch sich ihr Zustand sichtlich verschlechterte. 1992 wurde mit ihrer Restaurierung begonnen und dank der Spenden aus aller Welt gehen die Arbeiten heute noch weiter.

En 1927, Aalto remporta le concours de la bibliothèque de Viipuri dont il ne commença la construction qu'à partir de 1934 bien que la conception se soit initiée en 1933. Les premières esquisses affichaient des lignes classiques prononcées mais le projet, exécuté des années plus tard, incorpora une nouvelle vision de l'architecture et se convertit en une œuvre majeure. Le bâtiment comporte deux volumes allongés qui se mêlent pour créer une zone commune accueillant l'entrée, les escaliers, visibles à travers une façade en verre, et le hall d'accès à l'auditorium, à quelques salles de lecture et à la bibliothèque pour enfants, d'une conception très attentive aux détails. L'éclairage des aires de lecture provient de claires-voies coniques qui tamisent la lumière. Ainsi, les lecteurs ne sont ni éblouis ni soumis aux changements brusques de lumière. Après la Seconde guerre mondiale, la bibliothèque fut abandonnée durant dix ans, se détériorant de manière prononcée. En 1992 germa l'initiative d'une restauration dont les travaux se poursuivent encore aujourd'hui grâce à des donations internationales.

Nel 1927 Aalto vinse in concorso per la biblioteca di Viipuri e, sebbene avesse cominciato il progetto definitivo nel 1933, il cantiere incominciò solo nel 1934. I primi schizzi avevano elementi marcatamente classicisti, ma il progetto che si realizzo alcuni anni più tardi incorporò un nuovo modo di vedere l'architettura e si convertì in un'opera maestra. L'edificio consta di due volumi allungati che si incontrano creando una zona comune in cui si trovano l'ingresso e le scale, visibili attraverso la facciata trasparente ed il vestibolo di accesso all'auditorium, ad alcune sale di lettura ed alla biblioteca dei bambini, che Aalto progettò con particolare cura per i dettagli. L'illuminazione delle zone di lettura avviene attraverso lucernai conici che selezionano la luce, in modo che chi legge non venga abbagliato o si trovi condizionato da bruschi cambi di luminosità. Dopo la Seconda Guerra Mondiale, la biblioteca rimase abbandonata per dieci anni e, a causa di ciò, soffrì un grave deterioramento. Nel 1992 venne promossa un'iniziativa per restaurarla ed i lavori ancora sono in corso grazie ai contributi che stanno giungendo da ogni parte del mondo.

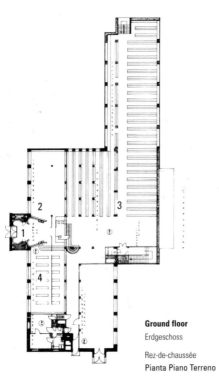

Ground floor

Erdgeschoss

Rez-de-chaussée

Pianta Piano Terreno

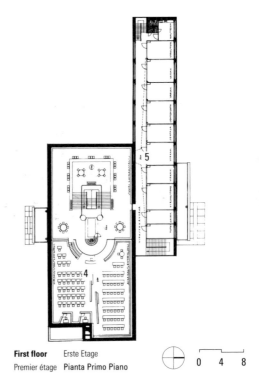

First floor Erste Etage

Premier étage Pianta Primo Piano

0 4 8

1. **Entrance**
2. **Vestibule**
3. **Books**
4. **Reading room**
5. **Classrooms**

1. Eingang
2. Vorhalle
3. Bücher
4. Lesesaal
5. Hörsäle

1. Entrée
2. Hall
3. Livres
4. Salle de lecture
5. Salles de cours

1. Ingresso
2. Vestibolo
3. Libri
4. Sala di lettura
5. Aule

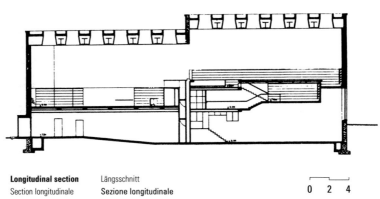

Longitudinal section　　Längsschnitt
Section longitudinale　　**Sezione longitudinale**

0　2　4

Villa Mairea

Noormarkku, Finland, 1937–1939
Photographers: M. Kapanen / AAM, Maija
Holma / AAM

In the nineteen-thirties, Aalto met the owners of an important lumber business, Harry and Mairea Gullichsen. This encounter led to the appearance of Artek, the company that manufactures and distributes the furniture designed by the architect. In 1938, the couple commissioned him with the construction of a summer house. This was done in red brick masonry, rubble, and wood. On the L-shaped ground floor, the common areas were within view of a small woodland clearing. In the intersection between the two wings of the house is the stairway leading to the first floor, where the private rooms are located. The house is built according to a series of contrasts: there are those that create the organic forms that hark back to a traditional Romantic architecture set against the straight lines of rationalism, or the warm wood finishings in the ground floor set against the plaster used in the bedrooms. Finally, the repetition of some leitmotifs in different parts of the house translates paradoxically into a rich, complex, suggestive project. The minute details that have gone into the building and the composition make Villa Mairea a classic of twentieth-century architecture.

In den dreißiger Jahren lernt Aalto die Besitzer einer bedeutenden Holzhandlung kennen, Harry und Mairea Gullichsen. Diese Begegnung führt zur Gründung von Artek, einer Firma, die die von dem Architekten entworfenen Möbel herstellt und vertreibt. 1938 beauftragt ihn das Ehepaar mit dem Bau eines Sommerhauses aus Ziegeln, Mauerwerk und Holz. Im L-förmigen Erdgeschoss wurden die gemeinschaftlichen Bereiche entlang einer kleinen Waldlichtung gruppiert. Am Schnittpunkt der beiden Flügel befindet sich die Treppe zur oberen Etage, in der die Privaträume liegen. Die Wohnung wird von mehreren Gegensätzen beherrscht, z. B. durch den Kontrast der organischen, nostalgischen Formen einer traditionellen, romantischen Architektur und den rechten Winkeln des Rationalismus, oder den warmen Holzverkleidungen im Erdgeschoss und dem Gipsverputz in den Schlafzimmern. Die Wiederholung bestimmter Gesten in verschiedenen Teilen des Hauses vermittelt jedoch paradoxerweise den Eindruck eines vielfältigen, komplexen und anregenden Projektes. Die minuziöse Sorgfalt in der Konstruktion und in der Zusammenstellung des Projektes machte Villa Mairea zu einem Klassiker der Architektur des 20. Jahrhunderts.

Durant les années trente, Aalto fit la connaissance de Harry et Mairea Gullichsen, les propriétaires d'une scierie. Cette rencontre fut à l'origine de la création de Artek, l'entreprise fabricant et distribuant les meubles conçus par l'architecte. En 1938, le couple lui confia l'édification d'une résidence d'été construite en brique, en maçonnerie et en bois. Le rez-de-chaussée, en forme de L, accueille les zones communes à l'orée d'une petite éclaircie du bois. L'intersection des deux ailes abrite l'escalier qui monte au premier étage, où se situent les pièces privées. La demeure est régie par divers contrastes. Ainsi ceux créés par les formes organiques réminiscentes d'une architecture traditionnelle romantique confrontée aux angles droits propres du rationalisme. Ou la chaleur de la finition en bois du rez-de-chaussée face au plâtre des chambres. D'un autre côté, la répétition d'éléments précis dans plusieurs parties de la maison propose, de façon paradoxale, un projet riche, complexe et suggestif. L'attention minutieuse de la construction et de la composition du projet ont converti la Villa Mairea en un classique de l'architecture du vingtième siècle.

Negli anni Trenta, Aalto conosce i proprietari di un'importante società produttrice di legname, Harry e Mairea Gullichsen. Quest'incontro diede luogo all'apparizione di Artek, la ditta che fabbrica e distribuisce i mobili disegnati dall'architetto. Nel 1938, la coppia lo incaricò della progettazione di una casa estiva che si costruì in mattoni, pietra e legno. Nel pianterreno, che possiede la forma di una L, si disposero le zone comuni, a fianco di una piccola radura del bosco. L'intersezione tra le due ali accoglie la scala che sale al primo piano, dove si collocarono le stanze private. La villa è dominata da alcune contrapposizioni, come quella tra le forme organiche reminiscenza dell'architettura tradizionale romantica e l'angolo retto proprio del razionalismo, oppure tra le calde finiture in legno del pianterreno ed il gesso utilizzato per i dormitori. D'altro canto, la ripetizione di alcuni gesti in differenti parti della casa ci restituisce paradossalmente un progetto ricco, complesso e suggestivo. La cura minuziosa nella realizzazione e nella definizione del progetto fece sì che Villa Marea diventasse un classico dell'Architettura del XX Secolo.

Site sketch   Skizze des Lageplans

Esquisse de situation   Schizzo della situazione

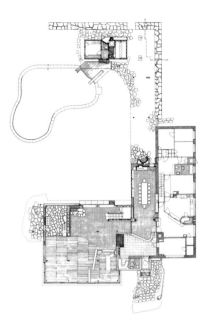

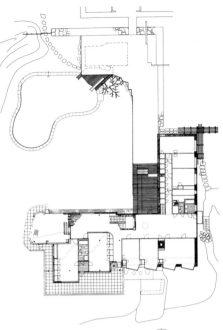

Ground floor   Erdgeschoss
Rez-de-chaussée   Pianta Piano Terreno

First floor   Erste Etage
Premier étage   Pianta Primo Piano

0   2   4

Baker House

Senior Dormitory for MIT, 362 Memorial Drive
Cambridge, Massachusetts, USA, 1946
Photographer: Jari Jetsonen / AAM

The Baker Dormitory is on the campus of the Massachusetts Institute of Technology (MIT), where Aalto worked as a guest professor when he was commissioned with the construction of a residence hall for students near the Charles River. The serpentine form of the building obeys the desire to orientate the maximum number of rooms toward the south. Moreover, the arrangement of the rooms with oblique angles avoids direct views of the bustling, noisy avenue on which the dorm is located. The northern part of the piece is used almost exclusively as complementary spaces such as halls, maintenance closets, and the unique fan-shaped elevator system. The structure was raised using bricks with different firing times so that the façade has a peculiar texture. Aalto had foreseen covering the masonry with climbing plants, but this idea was abandoned for budgetary reasons. The cafeteria block and that of the restaurant are of gray marble lighted by cylindrical skylights. The rooms are furnished in designs by Aino Aalto manufactured by Artek.

Das Wohnheim Baker befindet sich im Campus des Massachusetts Institute of Technologie (MIT), an dem Aalto als Gastprofessor arbeitete als er mit dem Bau eines Studentenwohnheims in der Nähe des Flusses Charles beauftragt wurde. Das schlangenförmige Aussehen des Gebäudes entspringt der Absicht, möglichst viel Zimmer nach Süden hin zu orientieren. Außerdem wird durch die Anordnung der Räume mit schrägen Winkeln die direkte Einsicht vermieden und der Lärm der lebhaften Straße, an der das Wohnheim liegt, gemildert. Der obere Teil des Gebäudes ist fast ausschließlich für zweitrangige Räumlichkeiten, wie z. B. für Gänge, Abstellräume und für die einmalige fächerförmige Treppe bestimmt. Das Gebäude wurde mit ungleichmäßig gebrannten Ziegeln gebaut, die der Fassade eine ganz besondere Textur verleihen. Aalto hatte ursprünglich vor, die Ziegel mit Kletterpflanzen zu verdecken; diese Idee wurde letztlich jedoch aus wirtschaftlichen Gründen abgelehnt. Café und Restaurant sind in grauem Marmor gehalten und werden durch zylindrische, an der ebenen Decke angeordnete Oberlichter beleuchtet. Das Mobiliar der Zimmer wurde von Aino Aalto entworfen und von Artek hergestellt.

Le dortoir Baker se situe sur le campus du Massachusetts Institute of Technology (MIT), où Aalto était professeur invité lorsque lui fut confiée la construction d'une résidence pour étudiants, près de la rivière Charles. La forme sinueuse du bâtiment obéit à la volonté d'orienter un nombre maximal de chambres vers le sud. De plus, la disposition des pièces, avec des angles obliques, évite les vis-à-vis et le bruit du tumulte de l'avenue où se trouve la résidence. La partie nord de la construction est destinée quasi exclusivement aux espaces secondaires, comme les couloirs, les salles de toilette et le singulier système d'escaliers en forme d'éventail. Le bâtiment est constitué de briques, cuites de façon irrégulière, ce qui confère à la façade une texture si particulière. Aalto avait prévu de couvrir les briques de plantes grimpantes, l'idée étant abandonnée pour des motifs économiques. Le volume qui accueille la cafétéria et le restaurant est en marbre gris et s'illumine à l'aide de claires-voies cylindriques disposées sur le toit plan. Les meubles des chambres ont été conçus par Aino Aalto et fabriqués par Artek.

Il dormitorio Baker è ubicato nel campus del Massachusets Institute of Technology (MIT), istituto nel quale Aalto era professore invitato quando lo incaricarono per la realizzazione di una residence per studenti vicino al fiume Charles. La forma serpenteggiante dell'edificio risponde alla volontà di orientare maggior numero possibile di stanze verso sud. Inoltre, questa disposizione crea angoli obliqui che evitano la vista diretta e il rumore della trafficata via su cui si affaccia l'edifico. La parte nord del complesso è destinata esclusivamente a spazi secondari come corridoi, sgabuzzini, e il singolare sistema di scale che ha la forma di un ventaglio. L'edificio è in mattoni di differente cottura, e questa scelta progettuale fa sì che la facciata acquisisca una particolare texture. Aalto aveva previsto di coprire il mattone con piante arrampicanti, alla fine però dovette abbandonare l'idea per questioni economiche. Il volume che accoglie il bar e il ristorante è in marmo grigio ed è illuminato mediante lucernari cilindrici disposti nella copetrua piana. Il mobiliario delle stanze fu disegnato da Aino Aalto e fabbricato da Artek.

1. Entrance	1. Eingang
2. Vestibule	2. Vorhalle
3. Rooms	3. Zimmer
4. Lounges	4. Aufenthaltsräume
5. Cafeteria	5. Café
6. Terrace	6. Terrasse
7. Dining room	7. Speisesaal
8. Kitchen	8. Küche

1. Entrée	1. Entrata
2. Hall	2. Atrio
3. Chambres	3. Stanze
4. Salons	4. Soggiorno
5. Cafétéria	5. Bar
6. Terrasse	6. Terrazza
7. Salle à manger	7. Sala da pranzo
8. Cuisine	8. Cucina

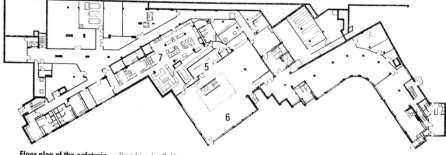

Floor plan of the cafeteria Grundriss des Cafés
Niveau de la cafétéria **Pianta del bar**

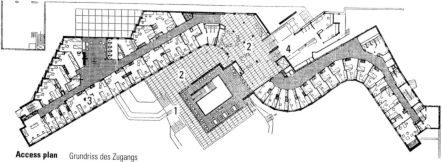

Access plan Grundriss des Zugangs
Niveau d'accès **Pianta di ingresso**

Floor plan of the rooms Grundriss der Zimmer
Niveau des chambres **Pianta delle stanze da letto**

0 4 8

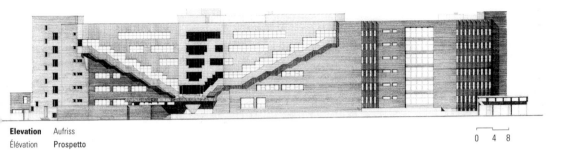

Elevation Aufriss
Élévation Prospetto

0 4 8

Säynätsalo Town Hall

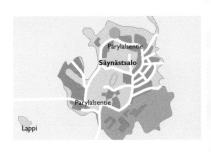

Säynätsalo, Finland
1949–1952
Photographers: M. Kapanen / AAM, Maija Holma /
AAM, Rune Snellman / AAM

**Aalto believed more in an indispensable local adminis-
tration, direct and effective, than in a national govern-
ment. To return to the town halls their lost monumentality,
the architect added to the initial program of the Säynätsalo council building a library, a commercial area, and some
living quarters. One of the problems that was dealt with
was the need to dedicate a large part of the surface area
to the tax administration, thus risking an office building
appearance. Aalto's solution was to put the town hall in
an edifice whose salient forms would mark its difference.
The whole is made up of four wings arranged around a
patio. The apartments occupy one of these, the stores are
on the ground floors that give onto the exterior, and the
administrative and cultural offices are orientated toward
the patio. The interiors, including the furniture, the wood-
work, and the lights, were designed by the architect. The
material used outside and in some of the more important
rooms inside is common red brick.**

Aalto croyait plus en une indispensable administration locale,
directe et efficace qu'en un gouvernement national. Pour rendre
aux municipalités leur monumentalité oubliée, l'architecte ajou-
ta au programme initial de l'hôtel de ville de Säynätsalo une
bibliothèque, une zone commerciale et quelques logements. L'un
des problèmes qui surgit fut la nécessité d'attribuer une part
importante de la surface à l'administration fiscale, susceptible
d'imprimer à l'ensemble l'aspect d'un immeuble de bureaux.
Aalto résolut ce point en situant le conseil municipal dans une
construction aux formes singulières pour le mettre en valeur.
L'ensemble est formé de quatre ailes disposées autour d'un
patio. Les appartements occupent l'un des blocs, les magasins
se situent aux étages inférieurs donnant sur l'extérieur et les
fonctions administratives et culturelles sont orientées vers le
patio. Les espaces intérieurs, y compris les meubles, les char-
pentes et l'éclairage, ont été conçus par l'architecte lui-même.
La brique rouge a été privilégiée pour l'extérieur et quelques-uns
des lieux intérieurs les plus significatifs.

Aalto glaubte mehr an die Unentbehrlichkeit einer direkten und
zuverlässigen Lokalverwaltung als an eine nationale Regierung.
Um den Rathäusern die verlorene Großartigkeit wieder zurück-
zugeben, erweiterte der Architekt die ursprüngliche Planung des
Rathauses von Säynätsalo um eine Bibliothek, einen Ladenbe-
reich und einige Wohnungen. Eines der Probleme bestand darin,
dass ein Großteil der Fläche der steuerlichen Verwaltung vorbe-
halten werden musste, wodurch das Gebäude Gefahr lief, den
Eindruck eines Bürokomplexes zu erwecken. Aaltos Lösung war,
das Rathaus in einem Gebäude auffälliger Formen unterzubrin-
gen, um es hervorzuheben. Das erreichte er mit der Konstruktion
von vier Flügeln um einen Hof herum. Die Wohnungen liegen in
einem der Blöcke, die Geschäftslokale befinden sich in den Erd-
geschossen und öffnen sich nach draußen und die Verwaltungs-
und kulturellen Funktionen sind auf den Hof hin orientiert. Die
Innenräume einschließlich der Möbel, Tischlerarbeiten und
Beleuchtung wurden von dem Architekten selbst entworfen. Für
die Außenverkleidung und für einige der repräsentativen Innenräume wurden rote Ziegel verwendet.

Aalto credeva maggiormente in una indispensabile ammi-
nistrazione locale, diretta ed efficace, che in un governo
nazionale. Per restituire ai comuni la monumentalità che
avevano perso, l'architetto aggiunse al programma inizia-
le del municipio di Säynätsalo una biblioteca, una zona
commerciale ed alcune residenze. Uno dei problemi che
dovette risolvere fu quello di dedicare necessariamente
gran parte della superficie disponibile ai locali dell'ammi-
nistrazione fiscale, con il risultato che il complesso
rischiava sempre più di sembrare un edificio per uffici. La
soluzione di Aalto fu quella di ubicare il municipio in un
edificio dalle forme singolari, in modo che potesse distin-
guersi. L'intervento si articola secondo quattro ali disposte
intorno ad un cortile. Gli appartamenti occupano uno dei
blocchi, i negozi si situano nei piani terreni rivolti verso l'e-
sterno e le funzioni amministrative e culturali si orientano
in direzione del patio.

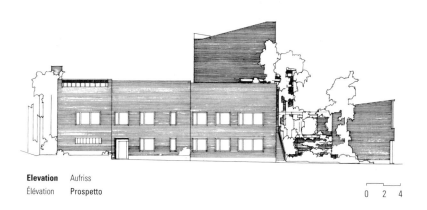

Elevation Aufriss
Élévation Prospetto

0 2 4

Plan Grundriss
Niveau Pianta

 0 3 6

Experimental House

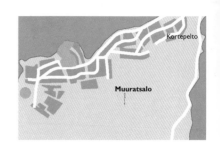

Melalanneltie 2
Muuratsalo, Aäynätsalo, Finland
1952–1954
Photographers: M. Kapanen / AAM, Maija Holma /
AAM, M. Vatanen / AAM

The Experimental House is located on the eastern side of the Isle of Muuratsalo, on a site discovered by Elissa and Alvar Aalto during their supervision of the work on the Säynätsalo Town Hall, which is near the island. The rocky terrain is covered with colorful mosses and lichens and also populated by low shrubs and by trees, above all pines and birches. The L-shaped dwelling contains a covered patio open on the western and southern sides, with magnificent views of the lake. The façades incorporate numerous materials: some walls are of red brick, others are stuccoed, still others are divided into small panels covered in different colored ceramic or brick pieces. In spite of being a modest structure using leftovers from other sites, the varied treatment of these materials enriches the whole composition.

Das Experimenthaus steht am Ostufer der Insel von Muuratsalo auf einem Gelände, das Elissa und Alvar Aalto während der Leitung der Arbeiten im Rathaus von Säynätsalo, einem Ort in der Nähe der Insel, entdeckten. Das Gelände – voller moos- und flechtenbedeckter Felsen – ist mit niedrigen Sträuchern und Bäumen bewachsen, vor allem mit Pinien und Birken. Die L–förmige Wohnung umschließt einen gedeckten Hof, der sich nach Süden und Westen hin mit herrlichen Ausblicken auf den See öffnet. Die Fassaden bestehen aus vielfältigen Materialien: einige Flächen sind aus roten Ziegeln, andere wurden vergipst und wieder andere sind in kleine Paneele unterteilt, die mit Keramikstücken oder Ziegeln in verschiedenen Tönungen verkleidet wurden. Obwohl es sich um ein eher bescheidenes Haus handelt, bei dem übriggebliebene Materialien von anderen Baustellen verwendet wurden, bereichert deren verschiedenartiger Einsatz die Wirkung des Gesamteindruckes.

La Maison expérimentale est située sur la rive est de l'île de Muuratsalo, sur un terrain découvert par Elissa et Alavar Aalto lors de la supervision des travaux de la municipalité de Säynätsalo, une localité proche de l'île. Recouvert de roches aux mousses et lichens multicolores, le terrain est peuplé de petits arbustes et arbres, essentiellement des pins et des bouleaux. La maison, en forme de L, enceint un patio couvert qui s'ouvre au sud et à l'est avec des vues magnifiques sur le lac. Les façades incorporent de nombreux matériaux : certains pans sont en brique rouge, d'autres en plâtre et d'autres, enfin, constitués de petits panneaux recouverts de pièces de céramique ou de brique aux tons divers. Bien que la construction soit modeste et fruit de la mise à profit de matériaux de récupération d'autres œuvres, le traitement varié de ces pièces a enrichi la composition de l'ensemble.

La casa sperimentale è ubicata sulla riva est dell'isola di Muuratsalo, in un posto che Elissa e Alvar Aalto scoprirono mentre stavano dirigendo il cantiere del municipio di Säynätsalo, località vicina all'isola. Il terreno – pieno di rocce ricoperte di muschi e licheni multicolori – è caratterizzato da arbusti bassi ed alberi, soprattutto pini e betulle. L'abitazione, a forma di L, si raccoglie attorno ad un cortile coperto che si apre a sud a ad ovest, con alcune magnifiche viste in direzione del lago. Le facciate incorporano numerosi materiali: alcune cortine sono di mattone rosso, altre sono ingessate, altre ancora sono composte da piccoli pannelli ricoperti da elementi ceramici o mattoni di tonalità differenti. Nonostante sia un edificio modesto in cui si utilizzarono materiali che erano avanzati da cantieri precedenti, la varietà compositiva con cui questi furono utilizzati arricchisce il valore del manufatto.

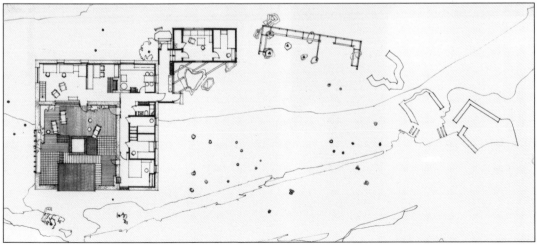

Plan Grundriss
Niveau Pianta

0   2   4

Church of the Three Crosses

Ruokolahdentie, 27
Vuoksenniska, Finland
1955–1958
Photographer: M. Kapanen / AAM

The conception of ecclesiastical spaces on Aalto's part always involved novelty. Already in the nineteen-twenties he designed churches that went beyond the typical structure, made up of a rectangular nave and a bell tower at one end. Clients used to more conservative views sometimes preferred to leave the buildings at the blueprint stage, but over the course of his professional career Aalto built numerous churches, chapels, and mortuaries. One of the best examples is the Vuoksenniska church, popularly called the Church of the Three Crosses. The religious works of the fifties and sixties typically show an acute sculptural tendency in which ornamentation disappears and the form of the building itself embellishes and gives character to the whole. The aim in this project was to create a flexible space that could serve as both church and social center. Aalto planned three consecutive rooms separated by moveable dividers so that the varying shapes can be used in different capacities.

Aaltos Gestaltung kirchlicher Räumlichkeiten überraschte immer wieder durch seine ungewöhnliche Konzeption. Bereits in den zwanziger Jahren entwarf er Kirchen, deren Struktur sich weit von der traditionellen Auffassung entfernte; sie bestanden aus einem rechteckigen Hauptschiff mit einem Glockenturm am Ende. Obwohl sich zuweilen seine Kunden mit ihrer weitgehend konservativen Vorstellung nicht an seine Projekte heranwagten, baute Aalto im Verlauf seiner beruflichen Tätigkeiten unzählige Kirchen, Kapellen und Bestattungsinstitute. Ein hervorstechendes Beispiel hierfür ist die Kirche von Vuoksenniska, im Volksmund die Kirche zu den Drei Kreuzen genannt. Die religiösen Bauten der fünfziger und sechziger Jahre zeigen eine eindeutige Tendenz zur Bildhauerei, die Ornamente verschwinden und an ihre Stelle treten die eigentlichen Formen des Gebäudes, die es verschönen und seinen eigenen Charakter herausstellen. Ziel dieses Projektes war die Schaffung eines flexiblen Raumes, der sowohl als Kirche als auch als gesellschaftliches Zentrum dienen sollte. Aalto entwarf drei aufeinanderfolgende, durch bewegliche Zwischenwände getrennte Räume, um so eine variable Gestaltung für unterschiedliche Funktionen und Kapazitäten schaffen zu können.

La conception des espaces ecclésiastiques par Aalto fut toujours novatrice. Il dessinait déjà au cours des années vingt des églises s'éloignant de la structure typique, formée d'une nef rectangulaire et d'un clocher à l'une des extrémités. Bien que ses clients aient parfois été très conservateurs, ils laissèrent libre cours à ses projets, Aalto construisant au long de sa carrière professionnelle nombre d'églises, de chapelles et de funérariums. L'église de Vuoksenniska, nommée communément Église des Trois Croix, en est l'un des meilleurs exemples. Les œuvres religieuses des années cinquante et soixante se caractérisent par une tendance sculpturale prononcée : les ornements disparaissent et ce sont les formes propres de l'édifice qui l'embellissent et personnalisent l'ensemble. Ce projet avait pour objet la création d'un espace flexible pour servir à la fois d'église et de centre social. Aalto dessina trois lieux consécutifs séparés par des partitions mobiles, la configuration variable pouvant ainsi absorber des fonctions et des capacités distinctes.

La concezione di Aalto degli spazi ecclesiastici fu sempre innovativa. Già negli anni Venti disegnò chiese che si distaccavano di molto dalla loro forma tipica, vale a dire dalla navata rettengolare e dala torre campanaria collocata in uno degli estremi. Anche se i clienti erano per mentalità abbastanza conservatori, non osavano controbattere il progettista che, lungo tutta la sua carriera professionale, costruì numerose chiese, cappelle e obitori. Uno dei migliori esempi è la chiesa di Vuoksenniska, comunemente chiamata Chiesa delle Tre Croci. Le opere religiose degli anni Cinquanta e Sessanta sono caratterizzate da una accentuata tendenza scultorea; scompare l'ornamento e sono le proprie forme della costruzione che abbelliscono e danno carattere al complesso. L'obiettivo di questo progetto era quello di creare uno spazio flessibile che avesse la funzione di chiesa e di centro sociale allo stesso tempo. Aalto disegnò tre stanze contigue separate tra loro da pareti mobili, in modo tale che i differenti spazi che si creano possano assorbire diverse funzioni e avere diverse capienze.

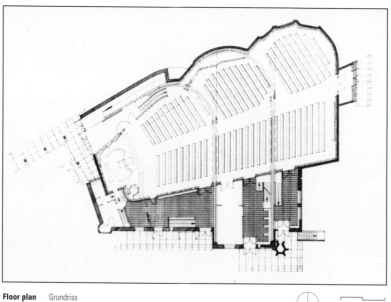

Floor plan   Grundriss

Niveau   Pianta

0   3   6

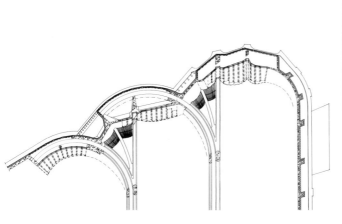

Detail of the structure in section   Detail eines Strukturausschnittes
Détail de la structure en section   Dettaglio della struttura in sezione

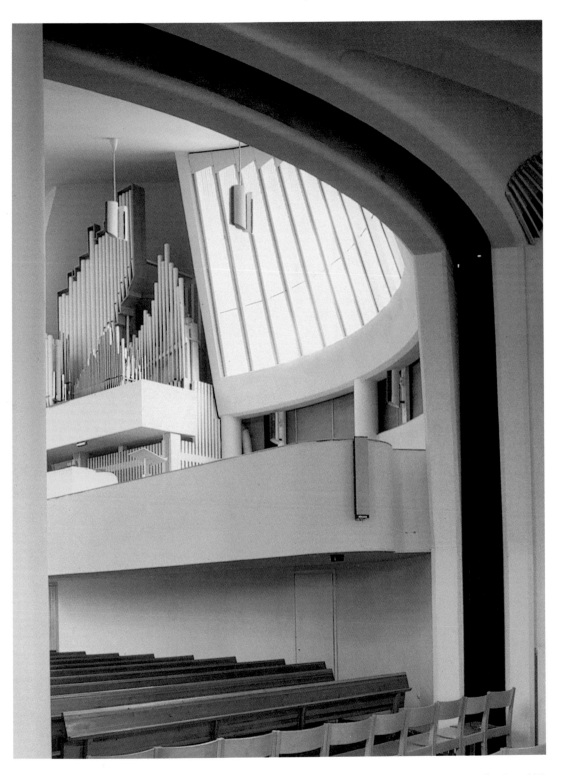

Main Building of the University of Technology

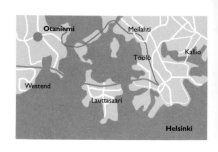

Helsinki University of Technology
Otakaari 1 X, Otaniemi, Helsinki, Finland
1953–1967
Photographers: M. Kapanen & Maija Holma / AAM

In the speech Aalto delivered on the occasion of the centenary of his school, he stated that the most important thing he had learned in his student years was to doubt, to use the capacity for forming a critical and independent opinion of doctrines and values. This faith in the individual would influence all of his educational buildings. A good example of this is the main building of the University of Technology in Helsinki, rising up in center campus, close to the library and some laboratory buildings. The construction is organized around a central tower that provides entry to a set of blocks arranged around small patios. The different wings house from two to four apartments as well as the administrative section of the university, the classrooms, an auditorium, and the Architecture Department. All of the parts of the building are planned to allow extension without damaging the original structure. The materials used are black granite and red brick in the façades and copper for the roof.

In einem Vortrag anlässlich der Hundertjahrfeier seiner Universität bestätigte Aalto, dass das Wichtigste, das er während seiner Studentenzeit gelernt habe, das Anzweifeln sei, die Fähigkeit einer kritischen, von Doktrinen und Werten unabhängigen Meinung. Dieser Glaube an das Individuum hätte alle seine Lehrgebäude beeinflusst. Ein gutes Beispiel hierfür ist das Hauptgebäude der Technischen Hochschule in Helsinki, das sich in der Nähe der Bibliothek und einiger Labors mitten im Campus erhebt. Der Bau ist um einen zentralen Punkt in Form eines Turmes angeordnet, der den Zugang zu einer Anlage aus Blöcken bildet, die kleine Höfe formen. Die verschiedenen Flügel sind zwei- und vierstöckig; dort sind die Verwaltung der Hochschule, die Aulen, ein Hörsaal und die Fakultät für Architektur untergebracht. Alle Teile des Gebäudes wurden so geplant, dass bei Erweiterungen die ursprüngliche Struktur erhalten bleibt. Die verwendeten Materialien sind schwarzer Granit und rote Ziegel für die Fassade und Kupfer für das Dach.

Dans son discours pour le centenaire de son école, Aalto affirma que l'enseignement le plus important qu'il ait reçu au cours de ses années d'étude fut celui du questionnement, du doute, de la capacité de former une opinion critique et indépendante des doctrines et des valeurs. Cette foi en l'individu allait influencer toutes ses constructions à vocation éducative. Le bâtiment principal de l'Université de Technologie, situé au centre du campus, près de la bibliothèque et de quelques laboratoires, en constitue un bon exemple. La construction est organisée autour d'une pièce centrale en forme de tour, offrant un accès à un ensemble de blocs groupés pour former de petits patios. Les différentes ailes ont entre deux et quatre niveaux et accueillent la partie administrative de l'université, les salles de cours, un auditorium et le département Architecture. Toutes les parties du bâtiment ont été planifiées pour qu'aucune extension n'endommage la structure d'origine. Les matériaux utilisés vont du granit noir et de la brique rouge pour les façades jusqu'au cuivre pour la toiture.

Nel discorso che Aalto fece in occasione del centenario della sua scuola, affermò che la cosa più importante che aveva appreso negli anni passati da studente era stata l'attitudine a formularsi delle domande, la capacità a formarsi un'opinione critica indipendentemente da dottrine e valori. Questa fiducia nell'individuo avrebbe influenzato tutti i suoi edifici di insegnamento. Un buon esempio di ciò è l'edificio principale dell'Università di Tecnologia di Helsinki, che si erge nel centro del campus, vicino alla biblioteca e ad alcuni dei laboratori. La costruzione si organizza attorno ad un corpo centrale a forma di torre attraverso cui si accede ad un gruppo di volumi che, nel loro insieme, vanno formando piccoli cortili. Le varie ali variano tra i due ed i quattro piani ed ospitano la sezione amministrativa dell'università, le aule, un auditorium ed il Dipartimento di Architettura. Tutte le parti dell'edificio si disposero in modo tale che un qualsiasi granito nero ed il mattone rosso per le facciate ed il rame per la copertura.

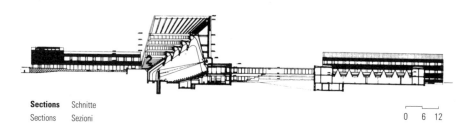

Sections   Schnitte
Sections   Sezioni

0 6 12

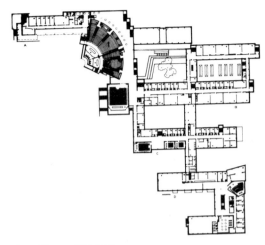

Semi-basement Souterrain
Étage semi-cellier Pianta Semi-interrato

Ground floor Erdgeschoss
Rez-de-chaussée **Pianta Piano Terreno**

0 4 8

Opera House

Essen, Germany
1959–1998
Photographer: M. Kapanen / AAM

After winning the competition for the new opera building in Essen, Aalto spent his time developing the project until the time of his death. The works finally got under way in 1981 under the supervision of the German architect Harald Deilmann, who based himself primarily on the drawings Aalto had left. The auditorium, which rises up off a park, is asymmetrical and can seat up to 1,100 spectators divided between the orchestra and three serpentine rows of balcony seats. This arrangement equalizes the distance between the seats and the stage and allows a good view of the onstage action. Also, thanks to the irregular floor plan, the auditorium never appears empty, even when few people attend. The walls are finished in warped aluminum panels that are both aesthetic and acoustic. This finish had originally been planned in wood, but was changed because of the fire risk. The ceiling, with a sound-permeable metallic mesh, acts as an optimal acoustic screen. The exterior facings are granite, the original white Carrara marble having been ruled out because it is susceptible to pollution.

Nachdem Aalto die Ausschreibung für die neue Oper in Essen gewonnen hatte, arbeitete er an diesem Projekt bis zu seinem Tod. Die Arbeiten begannen schließlich im Jahr 1981 unter der Leitung des deutschen Architekten Harald Deilmann, der sich weitgehend an die von Aalto hinterlassenen Zeichnungen hielt. Das Auditorium mitten in einem Park ist asymmetrisch und hat eine Kapazität für bis zu 1.100 Zuhörer, die sich zwischen Parterre und drei wellenförmigen Logenreihen verteilen. Diese Anordnung gleicht die Entfernungen zwischen Sitzplätzen und Bühne aus und gewährt eine gute Sicht auf die Vorführung. Dank der Unregelmäßigkeit des Raumes erscheint das Auditorium selbst bei wenig Publikum niemals leer. Die Wände sind mit gebogenen Aluminiumlamellen verkleidet, die sowohl eine ästhetische als auch eine akustische Funktion erfüllen. Ursprünglich war an eine Holzverkleidung gedacht worden, was aber wegen Feuergefährlichkeit abgelehnt wurde. Die Decke, ein schalldurchlässiges Metallnetz, wird zu einer optimalen akustischen Abschirmung. Die Fassaden sind aus Granit, da weißer Carrara-Marmor wegen seiner leichten Verschmutzung ausgeschlossen wurde.

Après avoir remporté le concours pour le nouvel édifice de l'Opéra de Essen, Aalto développa le projet jusqu'à la fin de ses jours. L'ouvrage commencé finalement en 1981, sous la supervision de l'architecte allemand Harald Deilmann, en se fondant essentiellement sur les dessins laissés par Aalto. L'auditorium, érigé dans le parc, est asymétrique et peut accueillir près de 1.100 spectateurs, se répartissant entre l'orchestre et trois rangs de balcons aux formes sinueuses. Cette disposition équilibre les distances entre les sièges et la scène et offre une bonne vision du spectacle. De plus, grâce à l'irrégularité du niveau, l'auditorium ne semble pas vide même si l'affluence n'est pas au rendez-vous. Les murs sont vêtus de panneaux d'aluminium déformés, répondant à des fonctions esthétique et acoustique. Cet habillage avait été projeté en bois, mais l'option fut repoussée en raison des risques d'incendie. Le toit, disposant d'un réseau métallique perméable au son, se transforme en un écran acoustique optimal. Les façades sont en granit, le marbre blanc de Carrare originel étant trop sensible à la pollution.

Il cantiere alla fine prese avvio nel 1981, sotto la supervisione dell'architetto tedesco Harald Deilmann e sulla base dei disegni lasciati dallo stesso Aalto. L'auditorium, che si situa all'interno di un parco, è asimmetrico e può accogliere fino ad un massimo di 1.100 spettatori, ripartiti fra la platea e tre file di paschi sinuosamente disposti. Questa disposizione uniforma le distanze dei posti a sedere dallo scenario e permette una buona visione dello spettacolo. Inoltre, grazie alle irregolarità della pianta, l'auditorium non sembra vuoto neppure quando effettivamente scarsa è l'affluenza del pubblico. Le pareti sono rivestite con pannelli curvi di alluminio che hanno utilità estetica ed acustica. Tale rivestimento era stato originariamente progettato in legno, ma si decise di abbandonare questa opzione a causa del rischio di incendi. Il tetto, con una rete metallica acusticamente permeabile, si converte in un ottimo schermo acustico. Le facciate sono di granito, dal momento che si abbandonò l'originale utilizzo del marmo bianco di Carrara per le sua oggettiva difficoltà a mantenersi indenne dall'inquinamento atmosferico.

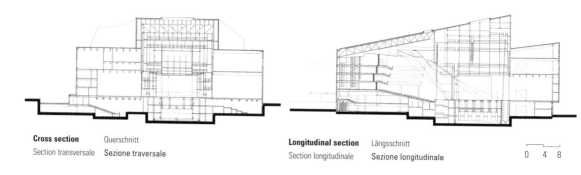

Cross section   Querschnitt

Section transversale   **Sezione traversale**

Longitudinal section   Längsschnitt

Section longitudinale   **Sezione longitudinale**

0 4 8

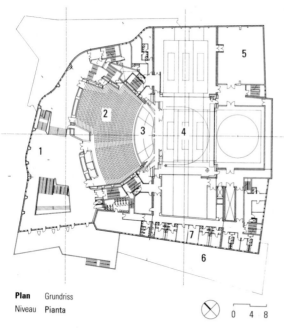

1. Vestibule	1. Eingangshalle
2. Orchestra seats	2. Parterre
3. Orchestra pit	3. Orchestergraben
4. Stage	4. Bühne
5. Storeroom	5. Lager
6. Terrace	6. Terrasse
7. Dressing rooms	7. Garderoben

1. Hall	1. Hall
2. Sièges d'Orchestre	2. Platea
3. Orchestre	3. Orchestra
4. Scène	4. Scenario
5. Réserve	5. Deposito
6. Terrasse	6. Terrazza
7. Loges	7. Camerini

Plan Grundriss
Niveau Pianta

0 4 8

Mount Angel Abbey Library

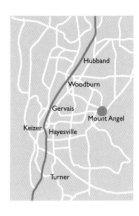

One Abbey Drive
Saint Benedict, Oregon, USA
1964–1967
Photographer: Jari Jetsonen / AAM

The Mount Angel Abbey Library building reflects and manifests the spirit and the concept of the clients: to build a library where the pleasure of reading would be combined with the efficiency and functionalism of a competent and specialized learning center. An extensive shelf system appears to configure the structure and the organization. The building contains studio rooms and reading tables distributed on three rooms with good natural lighting. The sensitivity that directed the project has also guided the re-plantation of all of the trees conserved from the site. In spite of the unique location on a pretty wooded hillside, the views never worried Aalto. He relegated them to strategic vantage points far from the reading areas so as not to distract the users. The interior/exterior distinction is manifested through the use of different materials in the façade and in the inside walls: brick, in one case, wood and plaster in the other.

Das Bibliotheksgebäude Mount Angel Abbey reflektiert und materialisiert den Geist und den Wunsch seiner Kunden: die Errichtung einer Bibliothek, in der der Genuss des Lesens mit der Nützlichkeit und der Funktionalität eines kompetenten und spezialisierten Lehrzentrums kombiniert wird. Die Struktur und die Aufteilung des Gebäudes scheint aus einem großangelegten System aus Regalen zu bestehen, mit Lernsälen und Lesetischen in den drei vom Tageslicht durchfluteten Stockwerken. Die Sensibilität, die in dem Projekt vorherrscht, erstreckt sich auch auf seine Einpassung in die Landschaft, wo alle Bäume des Grundstücks erhalten werden konnten. Trotz der einmaligen Lage auf einem bewaldeten Hügel schenkte Aalto den Aussichtsmöglichkeiten wenig Aufmerksamkeit; sie wurden auf strategische Aussichtspunkte weit entfernt von den Lesebereichen verlegt, um die Leser nicht abzulenken. Der Gegensatz zwischen Innen und Außen findet durch die Verwendung verschiedenartiger Materialien an der Fassade und bei den Innenwänden seinen Ausdruck: Ziegel für die Fassade, Holz und Gips für die Innenräume.

Le bâtiment qui abrite la bibliothèque de Mount Angel Abbey reflète et matérialise l'esprit et le propos des clients : créer une bibliothèque où le plaisir de la lecture se mêlerait à l'efficacité et à la fonctionnalité d'un centre éducatif compétent et spécialisé. Un vaste système de rayonnage semble donner forme à la structure et à l'organisation de l'édifice, contenant salles d'étude et tables de lecture réparties sur trois niveaux baignés de lumière naturelle. La sensibilité qui régit le projet a également guidé l'implantation dans le paysage, au cours de laquelle ont pu être préservés tous les arbres du terrain. En dépit d'une situation singulière, sur une belle colline boisée, les points de vue n'ont pas préoccupé Aalto, les reléguant à des sites stratégiques éloignés des zones de lecture afin de ne pas distraire les usagers. La différenciation intérieur-extérieur se manifeste également par l'utilisation de matériaux distincts sur la façade et sur les revêtements intérieurs : brique, pour l'une, bois et plâtre, pour les autres.

L'edificio che ospita la biblioteca Mount Angel Abbey rispecchia e materializza lo spirito ed il proposito dei committenti: erigere una biblioteca in cui il piacere per la lettura si combinasse con l'efficienza e la funzionalità di un centro di docenza competente e specializzato. Un grande sistema di scaffali sembra conformare la struttura e l'organizzazione dell'edificio, che contiene sale di studio e tavoli di lettura distribuiti su tre piani irraggiati da luce naturale. La medesima sensibilità che ordina il progetto guidò il suo inserimento nel paesaggio, per cui si poterono conservare tutti gli alberi che sorgevano nel lotto. Nonostante la singolare ubicazione in una bella collina alberata, le viste non preoccuparono mai Aalto, che le limitò ad alcuni punti selezionati lontani dalle zone di lettura, per non distrarre gli utenti. La diversità tra interno ed esterno si manifesta anche nell'utilizzo di materiali differenti nella facciata e nei rivestimenti interni: mattone in un caso e legno e gesso nell'altro.

Southwestern elevation Südwestlicher Aufriss
Élévation sud-est Prospetto Sud-Ovest

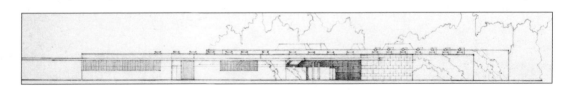

0 2 4

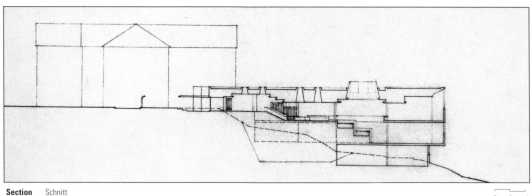

Section   Schnitt
Section   Sezione

0   2   4

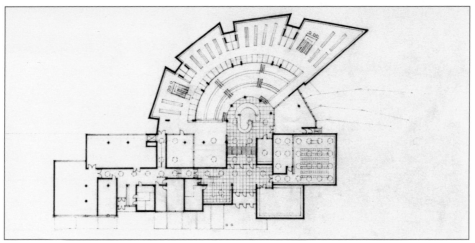

Plan Grundriss
Niveau **Pianta**

0   5   10

Furniture

Photographers: M. Kapanen / AAM, Maija Holma / AAM, Rune Snellman / AAM & Artek

Contemporary design is criticized for lacking exclusivity and for being overly influenced by fashions. Most furniture today does no more than adapt to a given setting, thus quickly becoming a collection of aesthetically obsolete objects. Alvar Aalto's creations, on the other hand, continue to have a traditional cut that is at the same time modern, going beyond the frontiers of style, taste, trends, or social classes. Furniture was another of Aalto's great achievements. Not infrequently, it was to serve him as a field of work and inspiration for architectural projects. The study and working of wood allowed him to come closer to a live, natural, organic material that offered him sensuousness and resistance, qualities that later found their expression in other materials like stone or brick. The work method of the architect and his team, creating prototypes and mock-ups in all the stages of the design process, brought into being objects that–in spite of being industrial manufactures–incorporated an artisanal stamp that conferred warmth and functionality. They are thus serviceable both in homes and in large public spaces.

Le design contemporain est critiqué pour son manque d'exclusivité et pour sa sensibilité aux modes. De nos jours, la plupart des meubles s'adaptent uniquement à un environnement déterminé et se convertissent finalement très rapidement en objets obsolètes. Les créations d'Alvar Aalto, en revanche, conservent un esprit traditionnel mais pour autant moderne, qui a dépassé les frontières du style, du goût, des modes ou des classes sociales. Les meubles ont constitué une autre grande réussite d'Aalto. Souvent, ils lui tenaient lieu de champ de travail et d'inspiration pour les projets architecturaux. L'étude et le travail du bois lui ont permis de s'approcher d'un matériau vivant, naturel et organique, offrant sensualité et résistance : des qualités transposées plus tard à d'autres matériaux, comme la pierre ou la brique. Le mode de travail de l'architecte et de son équipe, créant prototypes et maquettes à chaque étape du processus de conception, a engendré des objets qui, bien que produits industriellement, affichent un caractère artisanal. Celui-ci leur confère chaleur et fonctionnalité et les rend idéaux tant pour les logements que pour les vastes espaces publics.

Dem modernen Design wird fehlende Exklusivität und eine zu große Abhängigkeit von modischen Einflüssen vorgeworfen. Die meisten Möbel von heute passen nur in ein bestimmtes Umfeld und verlieren sehr schnell ihre Attraktion als ästhetische Gegenstände. Die Kreationen von Alvar Aalto hingegen wahren ihren traditionellen und gleichzeitig modernen Stil und überwinden die Schranken von Stil, Geschmack, Moden oder gesellschaftlichen Klassen. Auch die Kreation von Möbeln gehörte zu den großen Erfolgen von Aalto, die ihm oft als Arbeitsgrundlage und als Inspiration für architektonische Projekte dienten. Er befasste sich mit den Möglichkeiten und der Bearbeitung von Holz und kam so zu einem lebendigen, natürlichen und organischem Material nahe, das ihm Sinnlichkeit und Beständigkeit vermittelte, Eigenschaften, die er später auf andere Materialien, wie z. B. Stein und Ziegel, übertrug. Zur Arbeitsweise des Architekten und seines Teams gehörte es, in jeder Phase der Designentwicklung Prototypen und Modelle anzufertigen. Die so entstandenen Gegenstände werden zwar industriell hergestellt, verleugnen jedoch ihre handwerkliche Herkunft nicht, die ihnen Wärme und Funktionalität verlieh und sie gleichermaßen für Wohnungen und große öffentliche Räume geeignet macht.

Si critica il disegno contemporaneo per la carenza di esclusività e per la eccessiva influnza della moda. La maggior parte dei mobili di oggi si adattano solo in un ambiente determinato e si convertono in oggetti esteticamente obsoleti in un tempo ristretto. Le creazioni di Alvar Aalto, al contrario, continuano a mantenere lo spirito tradizionale e allo stesso tempo moderno che ha superato le barriere dello stile, del gusto, dela moda o delle classi sociali. I mobili furono un altro grande successo di Aalto, e spesso erano utilizzati come campo di lavoro e di ispirazione per i progetti architettonici. Lo studio e il lavoro del legno gli permisero di avvicinarsi a un materiale vivo, naturale, organico, che offirva sensualità e resistenza, qualità che avrebbe successivamente trasportato ad altri materiali, come la pietra o il mattone. Il modo di lavorare dell'architetto e del suo gruppo, creando in questo modo un prototipo in tutte le tappe del disegno, dette luogo a oggetti, che anche se erano prodotti dell'industria, incorporavano un marchio artigiano in tutte le tappe del processo della creazione che conferiva qualità e funzionalità, in tutto quello che riguradava residenze come i grandi spazi pubblici.

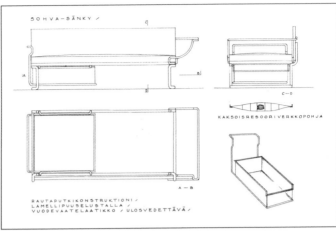

SOHVA—SÄNKY /

KAKSOISRESOORIVERKKOPOHJA

RAUTAPUTKIKONSTRUKTIONI /
LAMELLIPUUSELUSTALLA /
VUODEVAATELAATIKKO / ULOSVEDETTÄVÄ /

Plan, elevation, and section of a sofa   Grundriss, Aufriss und Schnitt eines Sofas

Niveau, élévation et section d'un sofa   Pianta, prospetto e sezione di un sofà

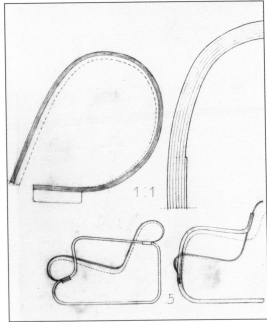

Construction details for a chair　Konstruktionsdetails eines Stuhles

Détails de construction d'une chaise　Dettagli costruttivi di una sedia

Chronological list of Aalto's major works

1919	Alajärvi youth association building
1920	Elementary school for Kauhajärvi
1921	Kauhajärvi bell tower and church
1922	Second Finnish trade fair in Tampere
1923	Restoration of Toivakka Church Chief Constable Karpio's summer villa, Jyväskyla Nuora House, Jyväskyla Terho Manner's house, Töysä
1924	Alajärvi Municipal Hospital Seinäjoki Defense Corps Building Jyväskyla Workers' Club Railway officials' block of flats, Jyväskyla Furniture of the Seurahuone Café, Jyväskyla
1925	Renovation of Kemijärvi Church Renovation of Korpilahti Church "Casa Laurén" , Jyväskyla
1926	Jyväskylä Defense Corps Building "Villa Flora", Alajärvi Muurame Church
1927	Officials' housing for Wilh. Schauman company, Joensuu Competition entry and project for SW Finland Agricultural Coop. Building, Turku Standard apartment block, the Tapani Building, Turku
1928	Turun Sanomat building, Turku Competition entry for Paimio tuberculosis sanatorium Furniture developed jointly with Otto Korhonen
1929	City of Turku 700th anniversary exhibition Paimio Tuberculosis Sanatorium
1930	ToppilaVaara pulp mill, Oulu Sets for play on Turku Finnish Theater Apartment Exhibition in the Helsinki Art Hall
1932	Fanshaped sauna, Paimio Villa Tammekann, Tartu, Estonia Karhulalittala glass design competition
1933	Viipuri City Library, final version

1935	Aalto's own home and office in Munkkiniemi, Helsinki

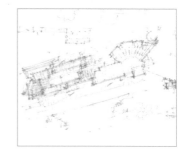

1936	Competition entry for the Finnish pavilion at the 1937 World's Fair in Paris Karhulalittala glass design competition Master plan and housing for Varkaus Master plan, pulp mill and housing for Sunila, Kotka
1937	Master plan and housing for Karhula Nordic Union Bank branch office in Karhula Master plan, paper mill and housing for Inkeroinen Furniture of the Savoy restaurant in Helsinki Villa Mairea, Noormarkku
1938	Master plan and housing for Kauttua Inkeroinen elementary school Three competition entries for the Finnish pavilion at the 1939 World's Fair in New York "Forest pavilion" for the Agricultural Exhibition at Lapua Aalto exhibition at the Museum of Modern Art in New York
1940	AA System standardized houses "Village of comrades in arms" in Tampere
1941	Regional plan for the Kokemäenjoki river valley Entrance to bomb shelter at Erottaja, Helsinki
1942	Master plan and lowrise housing for Säynatsälo
1943	Master plan for the Strömberg company's industrial estate and housing in Vaasa Master plan in Nynäshamn, Sweden
1944	"Reinder horn plan"for Rovaniemi Sauna in Kauttua
1945	"Negro Village" in Huutoniemi, Vaasa

1946	Artek pavilion in Hedemora, Sweden Villa Kauppi in Hirvisalo near Heinola Baker House, MIT, Cambridge, Massachusetts
1947	Master plan Imatra Villa Kihlman on Lake Näsijärvi Aino and Alvar Aalto exhibition in Helsinki, celebrating 25 years of collaboration
1948	Finnish Engineering Society building in Helsinki Säynatsälo municipal offices

1949   Town planning competition for Otaniemi, Espoo
          Säynatsälo Townhall

1950   Indoor stadium on the campus of Otaniemi, Espoo

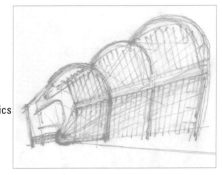

1951   Area plan, factory and housing for Tippi Oy, Oulu
          Competition entry for Seinäjoki Church
          Competition entry for Jyväskylä Institute of Pedagogics
          (later Jyväskylä University)
          "Rautatalo" commercial building in Helsinki
          Country club for EnsoGutzeit Oy in Kallahti, Helsinki

1952   National Pensions Institute office in Helsinki
          Experimental house on Muuratsalo island, Säynatsälo
          House of Culture, Helsinki

1953   Helsinki University of Technology Main Building, Otaniem
          National Pensions Institute housing in Munkkiniemi, Helsinki

1954   Master plan, paper mill and housing for EnsoGutzeit Oy in Summa
          Alvaar Aalto's studio in Munkkiniemi, Helsinki
          Apartment block in the Hansaviertel, Berlin, Germany
          Central Finland Museum in Jyväskylä
          The motor boat "Nemo propheta in patria"

1955   Finnish pavilion in Venice's biennale park, Italy
          Church of The Three Crosses of Vuoksenniska, Imatra
          Housing and businesscomplex "Sundh Center" in Avesta,
          Sweden Typpi Oy site manager's house "Villa Lehmus" in Oulu

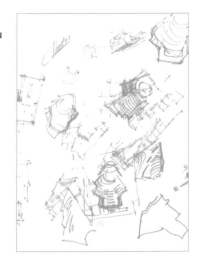

1956   La Maison Carré in Bazoches, France
          Korkalovaara housing area in Rovaniemi

1958   Wolfsburg Cultural Center, Germany
          North Jutland Art Museum in Aalborg, Denmark
          Competition entry for Kiruna Town Hall, Sweden
          "Neue Vahr" highrise block in Bremen, Germany

1959   Opera House and music theater in Essen, Germany
          EnsoGutzeit Oy headquarters, Helsinki
          Memorial of the battle of Suomussalmi, sculpture
          Power plant at the Lieksankoski rapids

1960   Enlargement of the Nordic Union Bank head ofice, Helsinki
          Church center in Wolfsburg, Germany
          Shoping center in Otaniemi, Espoo
          Power plant at the Pankakoski rapids
          Seinäjoki City Library

1961	Rovaniemi administrative and cultural center
	Seinäjoki City Theater
	Apartments blocks in Tapiola, Espoo
	The "Book Palace" (Academic Bookshop) in Helsinki
	Institute of International Education, New York
	Västmanland-Dala studentbuilding in Uppsala, Sweden

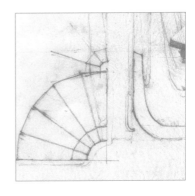

1962	Scandinavian House in Reykjavik, Iceland
	Institute of Physical Education, University of Jyväskylä

1963	Church center in Detmerode, Germany
	Row house in Jakobstad
	Student housing for the University of Technology
	in Otaniemi, Espoo

1964	Jyväskylä administrative and cultural center
	Schönbühl highrise block in Lucerne, Switzerland
	Office building in Seinäjoki
	Maison Aho, Rovaniemi
	Ekenäs Savings Bank
	University of Technology library, Otaniemi, Espoo
	Mount Angel Abbey Library

1965	Church center Riola, Italy

1967	Jyväskylä police headquarters
	Villa Kokkonen, Järvenpää

1969	Lappia multipurpose building, Rovaniemi
	Main Church in Lahti
	Villa Skeppet (for Göran Schildt), Ekenäs

1971	Alvar Aalto's Museum in Jyväskylä